Reflections
of the Heart

Charles Holmes

Reflections of the Heart

Copyright © 2018 Charles Holmes

Printed in the United States of America

Published by

Big Hat Press
Lafayette, California
www.bighatpress.com

Cover Painting | Watercolor
"Egret in a Cypress Swamp"
Nancy Ricker Rhett

DEDICATED TO

Rosalie Louise Gallick, my Mother,
and
Aidan Lee Elenteny

BOOKS BY CHARLES HOLMES

POETRY BOOKS

Streets That Speak*
For Understanding Eyes
Reflections of the Heart
Reflections of the Soul

*About streets that do not have enough and streets
that do have enough

NON-FICTION BOOKS

Hard Life, Kindness Ever Awake†
Thoughts From Millie**

**Interview quotes/practical wisdom from an elder
at 89, 90, and 91 years old

CHILDREN'S BOOKS

Bo Loney Goes to a New School
The Silver-lettered Poem in the Sky
The Cloth of 100 Wrinkles
Aidan Dreams Amazing Dreams
Aidan Dreams of 105 Fortune Cookies
Kid-like Poetry with a Bit of a Smile...Sometimes
Kid-like Poetry for Kids Who Are "Cool" at School
Kid-like Poetry for Kids Who Like Recess
Shy Kai Wished He Could Fly†

†In process

Available on Amazon

To contact author, please email rlg121212@gmail.com

CONTENTS

III

PREAMBLE

I am a poet because my dear mother was a poet. I am a continuation of her heart. My words are her words. I was also moved to write these last few years by my love for my surrogate grandson, 10 year old Aidan.

My formal and private study over many years has helped greatly guide my pen, along with suffering, hurdles, and substantial support.

I write to touch people's lives, that they in reading my work perhaps at times awaken a feeling, and gain a thought or two.

I

Grateful I

Candles that glow,

    streams that flow,

flat stones for brief stroll,

    all benefiting poetic soul.

Another Day

Early dawn
    before darkness announces day,
ruffled time,
    when mind wanders into tomorrow's corners.

Inmost spirit to walk into light,
    seek own peace,
go one's course,
    have an effect somehow.

Trail

Walk trail, scatter weeds,
       to open, not know when,
cottage, graceful temple,
       sacred walls and doors,
garden, jewel in the sun,
       artful bed of flowers,
sky looks on,
       with its unsolved mystery,
earth, awed nature,
       though jealousies in the brush,
journey's secret treasure,
       content of the person.

Reminder

Human spirit looks to sky,
    asks
who are you,
    who am I,

why do I not know the world,
    what does it do to the soul?

Possibilities within, without,
    accept today's sidewalk,
not to waste this time.

Bigger Heart

We all need a bigger heart;
      steps are still without one.
We all need to live in harmony
      with our core. That's the quest.

Joy to embrace that bigger heart,
      inner self linger close,
bathe in its sun,
      steps more mindful.

All to help us know who we are,
      accept where we are,
be in the moment, focus on
      what to get out of today.

Gratitude

Grateful for Time,
        old lanterns that shine,
understanding eyes of a few
        with hearts benign.
Good focus
        on what I can control,
healthy struggle
        towards noble goal.
Thinking possibilities
        in new way,
to add hopeful feeling
        to challenging day.

Centenarian's Ways

Asked about longevity,
     the centenarian of 102 said
"You've got to love your enemies."
     Another 106, noted
"I love to create."

     At breath's end
did they become
     the best possible person?

Beauty

Look for the beauty in life,
        concentrate on that,
walk beside it,
        have language for it,
reach for balance.

The Big Picture

Genetics, firm, steady, unchanging in the seasons.
Environment, flexible, hopefully friendly.
Soul-essence, unique interface
       between core and environment,
       which needs water and light,
       so that spirit can breathe well,
       uplift, prevail, wave happily.

Reflecting

I am a flower…glad to awaken a little joy on planet earth.

I am a tree…green art that listens and hears, observes and sees.

I am an ocean…happy that surfers roll with the waves.

I am a lake…enjoying place, misty air, sacred silence.

I am a fish…thirsty for good and freedom.

I am a bird…grateful for sheltered nest.

A Tree

Earthen statue with leaves,
      does more than shade, shelter, and spread,
never talks about sun, wind, cold,
      gives birds a place to rest,
may droop, but self-image strong and positive,
      turns different colors,
seems not to mind disheartening weather,
      graceful timber painted artistically,
those with entanglements, elegant art,
      profiles in courage,
storms come,
      are they forgotten?
anxious moments,
      how deeply felt?
doesn't waste time,
      accepts what doesn't change,
thankful for the bright side.

Into the Moment

What helps bring a great spirit
        into the moment,
meditation voice,
        feeling love at one's core,
centering on what truly matters,
        doing well what one does,
confident outlook smiling at dawn,
        being conscious of steps and words,
focusing on what one can control?

An Ordinary Day

Outstretched hand,
    opening door,
touching curtain,
    holding glass,
…simple art of an ordinary day.

Sifting sand,
    smiling at sunset,
skipping on broken sidewalk,
    glaring at bobbing boat
in freshly painted berth,
    …gentle art of an ordinary day.

Whistling stroll in drizzly rain,
    sprightly walk in untrodden woods,
meditating eyes gazing at still lake,
    wise steps making veritable footprints,
…subtle art of an ordinary day.

The dignity of demeanor.

Sidewalk Crack

Exquisite flower,
     from sidewalk crack,
to brighten busy day
     of hurrying feet,
not blessed with garden,
     clear pond, colorful pot,
just there
     for attentive eyes,
glanced at by some,
     unnoticed by most,
soft breathing,
     even in chilling wind.

Quest

Sense of self,
      uphill trudge,
experienced eyes squinting
      at fragile dreams,
enough support so big,
      conscious of
susceptibility to suggestion,
      valuing eager quest,
how to enjoy today?

Spiritual Things/Moments

Spiritual things:
  special old book
    quiet lake
  sentimental picture frame
      creatively written greeting card
  deep-cut, heavy, old glass
        craftsman-carved bookcase
  photo of loved one
      dawn
  sunset
    poetic words.

Spiritual moments:
  kitten on chair
      pup on sofa
  quiet forest
      wonderful rainbow
  singing stream
        inspiring mountain
  creative soul by the sea
      caring
  being there
        friend's love voice
  wise choice
        going medium slow
  4 year old saying
      "I love you."

Kitten

Kitten on stairway,
    soft stillness,
inner knowing,
    image of confidence.

Enjoying what one has,
    free movement,
quiet courage,
    fearless on the step.

Ready for the unexpected,
    present,
open to possibilities
    with steps always forward.

Love Air

Life, gift of time,
 gift of love,
where trees can touch stars,
 waterfalls baptize forests,
mountain peaks speak to sky.

Mind pictures soul as true source,
 invents future with imagining eyes,
feels light though steps in the dark,
 creates green garden with gates wide-open.

Soul breathes into deep stillness,
 centers on its sacred core,
rests there lightly,
 gives energy to where heart lives.

Refuses to look back,
 builds on the bright side,
focuses on what it can control,
 aglow in noontide sun, unfathomable night.

Sense of precious belonging
 on winding road to God-essence,
steady upward climb to self,
 grateful for love air providing the way.

II

Grateful II

Love voice
      at low tide,
the right word
      and the might of it.

Tranquility

How to be happy
    when dark clouds dominate fair sky,
coins at market harder to earn,
    too many on street corners with sad signs.

Not to wander in the woods,
    but define self in intricate forest,
clarify unique trail satisfactorily,
    move on serenely, in spite of mindless wind.

Treating weeds with care,
    growing oneself decision by decision,
asking deep down, is it enough
    that my breathing will help others to love.

Year Before Us

Year of important steps,
    kindness on trail,
squirrel unafraid to cross road
    for crumb or berry,
pigeon content in its way,
    seagull hovering high,
bird singing lilting tune,
    not victim of the storm,
kitten and pup toying with
    broken plaything.

Year of advancing steps,
    goodness rewarded
like never before,
    honor nodding at each day's sunset,
more than yesterday's calendar,
    character center stage,
each one's inner artist
    instinctive and unique,
even turning worry into creativity
    creating a masterpiece.

4 Leaf Clover

First leaf - home-bound birds,
        singing in soul-expanding sun,
even after drenching rain.

Second leaf - whispering trees,
        hinting strength, learning,
wisdom beyond their years.

Third leaf - healing waters,
        cleansing, rippling, calm, still,
flowing with turning stream.

Fourth leaf - verdant earth
        reaching skyward,
thrusting its native plants,

each a touch of hope
        in the worldly wind.

Mysteries

Where did I come from,
      where am I going,
who am I,
      where is home.

How long
      to learn
to accept
      meaningless reality?

Today

Thursday, Miracle Day; today is Wednesday,
blue sky, cool breeze, birds sing,
splendorous dawn, clear morning,
subtle magic behind wavering curtain.

Another day to be calm and strong in a gentle way,
knowing the content of the person
can be its own reward,
every wall can have a window.

Let honor intensify steps,
be true to heart,
sparkle under your star,
be attentive to what's around.

Lesson From a Delightful Dog

Have not 'arrived' socially,
     but Patrick, the delightful dog, likes me,
really gets excited when I open the front door,
     can't wait to be picked up.

Goes about his day,
     doing one thing at a time,
never tires of ragged doll,
     appreciates pillow, likes carrots.

Has freedom without a leash,
     doesn't seem to worry,
peace in who he is,
     enjoys what he has.

Silent Forest

Noiseless trees stretching skyward,
    seemingly sleepless, ageless,
unique loneliness,
    creating shadows,
gazing non-judgmentally,
    swaying calmly, listening carefully,
giving so,
    humble strength.

One can think about
    how much self-knowledge therein,
what deep vibrations when carved,
    sun bruising, storm battering,
yet inner beauty,
    silent wood speaking
with special indescribable grace.

Friends, Ritual, Prayer

Friends so vital, yet some become acquaintances,
    others, separate,
paths going distant ways,
    certain ones who drift away, mystery in the why.

Another help for a good week,
    vital ritual, plan for the day,
prioritizing to lift energy level,
    practical organizing way.

Then too, praying daily,
    believing it will have an effect somehow,
even though one might ponder,
    does it touch those without conscience?

Dancing

Dancing on traveled trails,
>which excel in beauty with elk, deer, wild ones,

on mighty sun-warmed boulder
>which has observed a thousand years,

near tranquil moon-lit waters
>that feel fish sensitive to life as few are,

with personal praying,
>bringing self into alignment with one's core,

spirit whispering to morning dawn,
>"Rivers speak; valleys doze; ridges stretch;

waterfalls thunder; hills charm,"
>inspiring small eyes in big ways,

joyous energy exploding,
>perhaps wondering what would have been

had dancing feet gone another way?

Plight

Newspaper —
    "Man Dies of Hunger"
(in the richest valley in the world)
    50,000 read.
How many feel?

What Will Be

When eyelids close,
     with there be a beautiful sight,
parents with open arms,
     encounters along the way
with welcome smiles,
     life's mysteries
bathing in light?

So Little We Know

Dawn, quick and gone,
dusk, rich twilight song,

path, sliding rocks, many times begin,
pebble, treasure amid the din,

magnet in a twig,
minutest splinter can be big,

natural forces, intelligent care,
nature, home of creation prayer.

Have Plan/Control It

Some want to capture your spirit,
    but you can hold on,
know when to walk away,
    not mar your day,
realize the fulfillment activities for you,
    appreciate what you have,
have gratitude each 24 hours,
    some live with lack of forgiveness,
not you,
    at times have to walk in the presence of evil,
accept what is and be awake,
    you can't control the system,
suffering comes from trying to change things
    you can't change,
look upon it inspired with ancient wisdom,
    simplify life,
find unconditional love people,
    do what makes you content,
manage discord as best you can,
    go to breath; try to be in the present,
challenge perceptions,
    don't feed into their anxious side,
have plan and control it,
    figure out long term options
and hope always.

Mind-Heart-Soul

When **mind** wanders,
    slips into wishful thinking,
strives for understanding,
    which at times is not enough,

heart needs a home,
    with hope at core,
framed with family, friends,
    caring, listening,

if lessened, **soul** suffers,
    might wonder,
has it met everyone it's meant
    to love?

III

Grateful III

Wise compassion,
    "cool head,"
courageous step,
    each a spiritual map.

Little Joys

What is the day's mighty note?
        goodness? honor? courage?
calm demeanor? love voice?
        gentle art? mindful ways?
or is it little joys?
        little joys?

Perhaps a Poet Can

A poet
can see flowers dance,
fly with soaring bird,
leap from cloud to cloud,
dream by the sea,
picture dying sun paint path in thick forest,
sense plight of sensitive star in dark sky,

hear a mother's whispering voice from beyond,
guide gentle guiltlessness to its art level,
be awake, alert, wise,
accept what is,
imagine the unlikely,
careful to respect
the fragile side.

Flow

Systems twist,
  mind turns
feet follow,
  path never imagined.

Thoughts wander
  through mist and fog,
spirit at times touching
  dabs of darkness.

Time-worn stories,
  complicated sentences,
notable metaphors,
  unwritten feelings.

Discord

Does every discord cut thin someone's garment,
     making sacred spirit fatiguing,
content of person hungering,
     sensitive feeling lessened,
good souls pierced,
     world a little less whole?
If it doesn't help,
     why so many bows stretched taut?

Seashore Art

On quiet shore
       resounding,
various shapes
       embracing sand,
simple art by the sea.

Precious Moments

We live in a world of monologue,
     dialogue with mirrors,
encounters from another time,
      the quest, to appreciate ones who hear us.

We go about our day,
     with many mindless steps,
hundreds of thoughts to distract,
      the quest, to appreciate ones who hear us.

Mountain

Majestic mountain
    deep heart within,
waiting patiently for climbers
    to recognize its singular soul.

Trees leaning outward
    without asking for help,
dynamic might there,
    calm confidence prevailing.

Trails, many,
    slight slips a-plenty,
protruding rocks, blind turns, hostile earth,
    all part of intriguing adventure.

Artistic feeling rising in air,
    dramatic symbols,
inspiration to those who live in valleys
    to look up with curious eyes.

In its time snow-covered peaks,
    skyward strength endures,
still offering cloaks of stone,
    supporting ridges of hope.

Water

Mystery of water
    far reaching,
its secrets unknown
    to mightiest star.
Makes earth smile,
    streams sing,
mountains cry,
    ocean hypnotize.
Language of its own,
    liquid existence,
maintains calm in devouring sun,
    feels rain drops' bright side,
copes with life
    in pond and puddle.

Haiku Poetry

1. Cherish the stern oak.
   It is yours for a lifetime.
   Water faithfully.

2. Believe in the sea.
   It is a treasure for you,
   as it is for me.

3. Forest before me,
   wood to build, fire to feed soul,
   grace in each splinter.

4. Thousand year-old rock,
   not recognized for its age,
   but living a dream.

5. Fire hypnotizing,
   mind warm and penetrating,
   blessing in the night.

6. Rose, sweet joyous red,
   emblem symbolizing life,
   thorns close, but love there.

Day by the Bay

Small boats bobbing,
     sails at rest,
wind artfully moving water,
     quiet Friday afternoon.

Hobby sailors
     tighten what needs to be,
doing what they enjoy,
     manifesting real friendship.

Young bikers ride by, energetic and graceful,
     eye "aquatic folks" controlling their day,
seemingly conscious of mooring's subtle art,
     clouds not matter.

Certain Spirit

If they realized a certain spirit
  in artist heart,
would they not
  want to create?

What pen would not find
  storied page,
what brush not refresh
  rickety canvas?

Time would be
  conscious moments,
stand on firm step,
  gaze beyond.

Oh Sea!

I love you, oh sea,
          especially,
when just you and me.

I love you, oh sea,
          you're better
than afternoon tea.

I love you, oh sea,
          more than
rest under a tree.

I love you, oh sea,
          tho forest, mountain, stream,
nothing like thee.

River

To discover self in narrowed waterway,
    precious moment,
as if encountering mirror
    with captions.

There, delightful dialogue
    speaks without language,
dipping into imagination,
    looking for magic wordings.

Gives light quiet hope,
    fresh ray to another miracle
that riverbanks said
    would not be.

Waters invigorate sensitive soul,
    perhaps asking,
what does a river feel
    when it goes out to sea?

The Path

Fear, opposite of love, gives you no power,
      go to breath; be mindful.
When things get out of control,
      breathe in, breathe out,
knowing its soothing power.

Tolerate what you can't change,
      find the LITTLE THINGS
you can control in your day.
      This, the path of personal freedom.
Remember, THE DAY IS FULL OF LITTLE THINGS.

Something Mighty

Day's work hard and long
      on planet which mourns for love,
struggling spirits
      looking for a little joy,
gentle art,
      unique touch,
conscious signature,
      prioritized interests,
single soul carves a day,
      hopefully finding in it
a mighty note
      which will say Yes to those hours.

IV

Grateful IV

To focus on
       what we can control,
on three things
       good about today.

Favorite Things

Things I like,
old books, quiet lakes, sleeping babies,
medium-sized waves, kitten on chair, dog on hind legs,
shopping organic, meditation ocean walk,
early dawn saying "Good Morning,"
love voice at low tide,
full tree breathing in urban parking area,
true friends, light rain, speaking sky,
penning a poem, sensing "I can do the task,"
finishing Saturday house cleaning,
exercise, sunset, smile from loved one,
silence's creative buds,
mother ever-watching, listening prayer soft and true,
sagacious insight, one's work well done,
feeling confident when it's time for another
New Beginning.

Moments of Beauty

How many touch the heart of a tree,
    find it breathing,
sense being part of it
    though they don't know the language,
reflect on footprints,
    imagine persons above the step,
wonder where they might be,
    no map to guide,
embrace a flower,
    breathe in its beauty,
feel its soul, then go another way,
    sometimes to recall,
true love is never wasted?

What Really Counts

Why look at a bell,
      it's the ringing.
Why look at a home,
      it's the belonging.
Why talk of finding a friend,
      it either happens or it doesn't.
Why talk of community,
      it either happens or it doesn't.
Why not listen to a tree;
      it has wisdom of the years.
Why not listen to the sea,
      it's always speaking.
Why not enjoy little joys more,
      they count so.

Difficulties

Difficulties help us to understand,
　　　　but not all,
far too many erode the pillar,
　　　　cut at core, stifle soul.

Sacred strengths
　　　　with mystery all their own,
hidden magic
　　　　bolstering spirit.

Spiritual way,
　　　　wisdom sometimes in wisp of cloud,
yet long, winding path asks,
　　　　do we really accept where we are?

Love Light

Even a tiny lamp gives to a room priceless sights,
    still shadows resting under pale air,
    painting a carpet awkward,
madly lined walls shouldering raw art,
    guilty cobwebs on narrow ledge rejoicing openly,
with gentle hope, flickering fondly
    at close of each dying day.

Old Souls know this, they see distinctly,
    hearing eternal tones echoing in air,
at peace within,
    their senses speak to apple trees,
skating children with staring eyes,
    seesaw players in disguise,
smiling flower with many sighs,
    listen to music carved on rock,
laughter in lyrical streams,
    dancing sounds of whistlers
who realize spirit of the walk,

look at themselves,
feel emotions which will change their lives,
forgive, experience the body responding,
realizing full well the power of one assured,
visioning their own well-constructed bridge,
facing privilege of work with determination,
climbing over what was once rugged wall,
on top gazing beyond,
magical intuition ever alive,

comprehending like no one else,
the room is important,
but the main thing,
how you choose to light it.

70 Years

We thought 10 was old,
        then came 30,
and of course, 40.
        How little we knew.

Now to see some things for the first time,
        there they were, waiting,
to touch a life,
        and make a difference.

So Much to Ponder

So many games,
  with many not realizing the one they're in,
they plod along taking in what appears to be,
  unwritten rules, deeply obscure, carving artfully.

Summer heat for all,
  with some flies staying too long.
Autumn, with more awareness,
  grateful for little things.

Winter ushers in movement medium slow,
  should there be applause, yet
who am I, where is home,
  where am I going?

Two Starting Anew

To piano their own music,
    a divine dance never to end,
loving gaze at family, overflowing
    into every part of walking and talking,
ready pen writing two lives,
    strong, steady, thoughtful,
in gentle search for accurate finds,
    youthful sensitivity, miracle smiles,
adult experiences becoming one,
    wisdom from ambling on winding sidewalks,
like growing oak reaching to the sky,
    contented, child-like maturity in its serene bearing,
living because of loving.

Each Dying Day

To clothe each day with honor,
    counting at least three little joys
that benefit living soul.

Be sufficiently there
    for those who enter my life,
intuiting, sensing the moment,
    feeling good about steps taken.

Do the day's tasks well,
    remembering that last hour
when one will wish
    they were done better.

Embrace nature,
    absorbing the connection,
touching earth and its offspring
    with a beauty-loving heart.

Pray,
    and hold that prayer
a thousand breaths,
    in gratitude for precious hours.

Fantasy Questions

In the desert, does wind write a plan in sand,
       near the shore, does the sea want to touch land,
in the forest, do plants look up or watch the trail,
       how does a cloud feel in a gale?

Can a stone enter into common discourse,
       do rocks ask why they are coarse,
do trees sensing they will not fall, give a big sigh,
       is there a welcoming door in the sky?

How Many?

On a planet with multitude of shadows,
    how many see their share of light,
feel enough enthusiastic emotions in the walk,
    sense sufficient wholeness of spirit?

    Perhaps close eyes,
        sit calmly,
    accept peacefully
        those with walled vision,

    prize honor,
        nurture it daily,
    with deep, moving heart
        that pierces life's absurdities,

    bathe in meditative waters,
        trusting in priceless hope,
    not drift like a log, but
        strive to address each human
    as a Thou.

Suffering

Realize deeply
      one's sufferings help others,
moving mystically
      like prayer and love.

Dynamic impact carries on somehow,
      arrives at a deeper understanding,
which once within a sea of mystery,
      now entrenched on verdant shore.

Hope

When darkness has reached its depth,
    turn doorknob, open,
see the room's light,
    find the door in the wall,
believe what you want to happen,
    knowing intuitively that
through failures,
    until the right thing,
when it's time.

Mysteries II

How can I ever know
        the difference I make
to those who enter my life?

Am I watched by those who are gone,
        with loving feelings, smiling eyes,
are there arms reaching out?

Am I loved by those unmet,
        ones I would have loved,
had hearts been given a chance?

What other way
        than to live each day
as well as I can!

ACKNOWLEDGEMENTS

Joan Arnott

Barbara Elenteny

Sheila Helms

Eliane McCaffrey

Rev. Bill McDonald

Nancy Ricker Rhett

MeMe Riordan

Aidan, grandson in heart, and the author

ABOUT THE AUTHOR

CHARLES HOLMES is an educated and creative soul. His perhaps most important work, *Streets That Speak*, is about streets that do not have enough and streets that do have enough. His poems in *Reflections of the Heart* and *Reflections of the Soul* offer moments for quiet consideration. His interviews in *Thoughts From Millie* are a collection of rich common sense from an elder at 89, 90, and 91 years old.

He is a surrogate grandfather to a 10 year old boy named Aidan.

He has delved into the magic of study formally and privately for many years.

He has created three recreation centers for children, has taught at two universities and one community college, has done social work with the elderly poor, and has authored two studies about their difficulties.

He also has written eight children's books (page v). Some are fun; others, sort of "cool." Still others are on the serious side.

He hopes that *Reflections of the Heart* conveys to the reader a feeling, as well as a thought or two.

To contact the author,
please email
rlg121212@gmail.com

Made in the USA
Middletown, DE
23 April 2022

64682435R00056